Matthew 24

Understanding its message for today-
Jesus is coming

Peter Michell

Index

Introduction

The events of Matthew 24

Chapter:

All bible references are from the New King James.

Introduction

When Paul wrote to the Thessalonians this is what he said:

'But concerning the times and the seasons brethren, you have no need that I should write to you. For you yourselves know perfectly that the day of the Lord so comes as a thief in the night.
For when they (the unbelieving) say 'Peace and safety,' then sudden destruction comes upon them, as labour pains upon a pregnant woman. And they shall not escape.
But you brethren *(the born again believers), are not in darkness so that this Day should overtake you as a thief. You are all sons of the light and sons of the day. We are not of the night nor of the darkness.'*   1 Thessalonians Chapter 5:1-5

Contrary to the teaching and thinking of much of Christianity we are expected to be and to become aware of the timing of the Day of the Lord.

He goes on to give a reason:
'For God did not appoint us to wrath, but to obtain salvation through our Lord Jesus Christ'   verse 9
'Put on the breastplate of faith and love and as a helmet the hope of salvation.'   verse 8
'Therefore comfort each other and edify one another, just as you are doing.'   verse 11

The objective and importance of the study of this difficult chapter is to bring the light of truth to an area where much misunderstanding abounds, thus bringing hope and comfort to believers.

Paul to Timothy:-
'Be diligent to present yourself approved to God, a worker who does not need to be ashamed, rightly dividing the word of truth.' 2 Timothy 2:15

The events of Matthew 24

To understand the chapter we need to grasp the outline of this period of time:

In answer to the disciples questions Jesus explains the following: (Some facts added from other scriptures.)

Today we are in the consummation of the age which includes -

Wars, rumours of wars, famines, pestilences, earthquakes – the beginnings of sorrows.

Then comes the rapture of the church – born again believers removed from the earth.

Then the tribulation -
Antichrist and a peace deal with Israel including the rebuilding of the Temple in Jerusalem

The abomination in the Temple and great tribulation
The world goes to war with Israel and the Lord

Jesus returns with His bride and defeats all His enemies at the termination of the age

The marriage feast of the Lamb on earth

The reign of Jesus in the millennium

Chapter 1
Matthew speaks to Jews and Gentiles

In the New King James Bible the introduction to the
Gospel of Matthew has this statement:
'Matthew is the gospel written by a Jew to Jews about a
Jew.'
The inescapable conclusion, having been reached by
Jesus genealogy, baptism, teaching, His miracles and
His death and resurrection - Jesus is indeed the long
awaited Messiah. Israel's King who will be coming
again to rule.

Gentiles are, by personal belief in Jesus, grafted into the
same root of God's favour as stated by Paul in Romans
11.

Although Israel rejected Jesus, nevertheless they can
and will be grafted again into the Olive Tree whose
root is fatness – the result of God's favour.

The disciples asked Jesus questions after He told them
that the Temple would be totally destroyed:
Tell us, when will these things be? And what will be
the sign of Your coming, and of the end of the age.'

We will look at His reply. It is helpful to bear in mind
Matthew's emphasis on Israel as we do as some of what
Jesus says applies only to Israel and not to His bride –
the born again believers.

A note about the Olive Tree of Romans 11

Some teach that the Olive Tree is Israel. The scripture describes Israel as 'natural branches,' not as the tree.

Born again believers (the true church) are not grafted into Israel but into the same tree and thus into the same root.

We, though coming from wild stock, become partakers of the root and fatness, or favour, of God pictured by the olive tree.

When Israel is restored it will be grafted back again into God's favour as natural branches.

Chapter 2
The chapter
(Printed here for ease of reference)

'Then Jesus went out and departed from the temple, and His disciples came up to show Him the buildings of the temple. And Jesus said to them, "Do you not see all these things? Assuredly, I say to you, not one stone shall be left here upon another, that shall not be thrown down."

Now as He sat on the Mount of Olives, the disciples came to Him privately, saying, "Tell us, _when will these things be? And what will be the sign of Your coming, and of the end of the age?_"

And Jesus answered and said to them: "Take heed that no one deceives you.

"For many will come in My name, saying, 'I am the Christ,' and will deceive many.

"And you will hear of wars and rumors of wars. See that you are not troubled; for all these things must come to pass, but the end is not yet.

"For nation will rise against nation, and kingdom against kingdom. And there will be famines, pestilences, and earthquakes in various places.

"All these are the beginning of sorrows.

"Then they will deliver you up to tribulation and kill you, and you will be hated by all nations for My name's sake.

"And then many will be offended, will betray one another, and will hate one another.

"Then many false prophets will rise up and deceive many.

"And because lawlessness will abound, the love of many will grow cold.

"But he who endures to the end shall be saved.

"And this gospel of the kingdom will be preached in all the world as a witness to all the nations, and then the end will come.

The great tribulation

"Therefore when you see the 'abomination of desolation,' spoken of by Daniel the prophet, standing in the holy place" (whoever reads, let him understand), "then let those who are in Judea flee to the mountains.

"Let him who is on the housetop not go down to take anything out of his house.

"And let him who is in the field not go back to get his clothes.

"But woe to those who are pregnant and to those who are nursing babies in those days!

"And pray that your flight may not be in winter or on the Sabbath.

"<u>For then there will be great tribulation</u>, such as has not been since the beginning of the world until this time, no, nor ever shall be.

"And unless those days were shortened, no flesh would be saved; but for the elect's sake those days will be shortened.

"Then if anyone says to you, 'Look, here is the Christ!' or 'There!' do not believe it.

"For false christs and false prophets will rise and show great signs and wonders to deceive, if possible, even the elect.

"See, I have told you beforehand.

"Therefore if they say to you, 'Look, He is in the desert!' do not go out; or 'Look, He is in the inner rooms!' do not believe it.

"For as the lightning comes from the east and flashes to the west, so also will the coming of the Son of Man be.

"For wherever the carcass is, there the eagles will be gathered together.

The coming of the Son of Man

"Immediately after the tribulation of those days the sun will be darkened, and the moon will not give its light; the stars will fall from heaven, and the powers of the heavens will be shaken.

"Then the sign of the Son of Man will appear in heaven, and then all the tribes of the earth will mourn, and they will see the Son of Man coming on the clouds of heaven with power and great glory.

"And He will send His angels with a great sound of a trumpet, and they will gather together His elect from the four winds, from one end of heaven to the other.

The Parable of the Fig Tree

"Now learn this parable from the fig tree: When its branch has already become tender and puts forth leaves, you know that summer is near.

"So you also, when you see all these things, know that it is near — at the doors!

"Assuredly, I say to you, this generation will by no means pass away till all these things take place.

"Heaven and earth will pass away, but My words will by no means pass away.

"But of that day and hour no one knows, not even the angels of heaven, but My Father only.

(Note* paragraph break moved here for clarity and new heading suggested;)

As in the Days of Noah.

"But as the days of Noah were, so also will the coming of the Son of Man be.

"For as in the days before the flood, they were eating and drinking, marrying and giving in marriage, until the day that Noah entered the ark,

"and did not know until the flood came and took them all away, so also will the coming of the Son of Man be.

"Then two men will be in the field: one will be taken and the other left.

"Two women will be grinding at the mill: one will be taken and the other left.

"Watch therefore, for you do not know what hour your Lord is coming.

"But know this, that if the master of the house had known what hour the thief would come, he would have watched and not allowed his house to be broken into.

"Therefore you also be ready, for the Son of Man is coming at an hour you do not expect."

*Paragraph breaks are not in the original text. No one knows the day or hour refers to the immediately preceding shortened tribulation, completing His answer to their questions.

Jesus 'next' thought starts with Noah adding more information and a sign that will be recognized by many of the 'left behind' Jews.

Chapter 3
The meaning of the two Greek words for 'end.'

As we come to un-wrap the passage, including Jesus answer to the disciples, a first step is to recognize that there are two different Greek words for 'end.'' The disciples question (verse 3) about the signs of His coming and the end of the age uses *'sunteleia'* for 'end.'

Jesus answer (verse 7) 'the end is not yet,' uses *'telios.'*

'sunteleia' has the meaning of the drawing together of the things that make up the end period. The word does not denote a termination but the heading up of events to the appointed climax. This period is known as the consummation of the age.

'telios' has the meaning – the termination, completion, the final issue or result of a state or process.

The meaning of the Greek words is taken from Vine's Expository Dictionary of Greek Words and Bullinger's Critical Lexicon and Concordance to the English and Greek New Testament.

Chapter 4
The consummation of the age

As we have seen in the last chapter this period of time covers the drawing together of those matters which need to be completed before the termination can come.

Chronological studies, beyond the scope of this study, tell us that this period started in 1933 when 2,000 lunar years were completed. (Please see 'The way of the moon and the way of the sun – the timekeepers' for details.)

The consummation period seems to last for 100 years, aligning 2,000 lunar years with 2,000 solar years from Christ's death and resurrection in AD 33.

So what has to be completed in this 100 year period?

The nation of Israel had to be reinstated – done in 1948 after a 15 year wait (1 chronological hour – could you wait with Me for 1 hour?)
Jesus said as a sign of His coming in Matthew 24, 'Look at the fig tree,' added in Luke 'and all the trees,' when you see them establishing and budding you know the time is near. Since 1933, when there were about 70 nations on earth, the number of 'trees' (nations) has now increased to over 200.

Israel was out of its land for 70 years as prophesied by Jeremiah and the reported in Daniel. Now are the 70 years being given back as one of the things to be completed?

The next matter to be completed before the termination is the 1 hour reign of the 10 kings of Revelation 17 which includes the reign of antichrist. The identity of the 10 kings is not disclosed and they will be likely to be spiritual beings as we find in Daniel 10. Here the prince of Persia defied the angel bringing God's message. The angel told Daniel the prince of Greece would follow. Whilst the two princes being described by the angel are clearly spiritual beings, nevertheless both the Kingdom of Persia and that of Greece had human manifestation and human rulers.

So we can see how the 100 year consummation of the age could be accounted for.

Jesus described this period in Matthew 24. Indeed our experience follows His warning – wars, and rumors of wars, famines, pestilences and earth quakes. The beginning of sorrows. Worse is to come for the Jews - they will deliver you to tribulation, and you will be hated by all nations.

The end (termination) is still to come.

Chapter 5
The termination of the age

The termination is sometimes referred to as the Day of the Lord, or the Day of His wrath. With this description the termination would be looked upon as a 7 year period leading to   ….

The climax, the final completion of the appointed matters which heralds the return of Jesus to reign on earth after the end of the tribulation.

Jesus return is explained for us in Revelation 19 where He is seen returning from heaven for the marriage feast with His bride - the born again believers who have spent the 7 years of the tribulation preparing as His bride in the place prepared for them in His Father's house.

Now we can understand that the 10 virgins waiting to go in to the wedding feast are not the bride. Rather they are religious ones still alive at the end of the tribulation. Those with oil have become believers during the tribulation, those without have not.

Now Jesus Millennial kingdom will be established on earth.

Chapter 6
Putting the message together.

Let's put the message of Matthew 24 into as simple language as we can:

First let's remove some confusion and some widely held interpretations that don't fit with the whole counsel of the scripture:

It is very widely held that we do not, and will not, know the timing of Jesus return.
This is then increased into we cannot expect to know and shouldn't even think of it. This view is based on verse 36 where Jesus is answering part of the disciples' question, *'when will these things be?'* (verse3) Jesus answers this part of the question with, *'but of that day and hour no one knows, not even the angels of heaven, but My Father only.'*
To know what Jesus was saying His statement must be read in the immediate context of what went before where He is warning of tribulation so awful that unless the time was shortened no one would survive. He is very clearly referring to the end of the tribulation after which He will return. – It is nothing to do with the rapture of the church, of which Paul tells us in 1 Thessalonians 5 – it won't come upon us as a thief in the night – we will be aware though we won't know the exact hour.
(The paragraph break just before verse 36 would be better placed after verse 36. – paragraph breaks and verse numbers were added later not being part of inspired text.)

Israel expected their Messiah but they failed to see that He would come twice – first as the suffering servant who takes away the sin of the world and later as the Messiah ruling the earth as the King of Kings. Soon to be fulfilled!

We are in danger of a similar error. Jesus comes to collect His bride and to take her to the place He has prepared in His Father's house for her, at the rapture of the church. (as promised in John chapter 14) Later He will come again to rule the earth as King of Kings and Lord of Lords (Revelation 19)

So here is the simple account –
The disciples are questioning Jesus after He tells them that the Temple will be destroyed.
'When will these things be, and what will be the sign of Your coming and of the end (consummation) of the age?'
His reply – lots of things are going to happen, don't be troubled by wars and rumours of wars, the end (termination) is not yet. More trouble is to come, famines, pestilences and earthquakes in various places – these are the beginning of sorrows.
Finally you will be hated by all nations and delivered up to tribulation, which becomes so awful that time has to be shortened for any to survive. (Remember Matthew's emphasis on the Jews! – the church has the promise that we are not subject to this wrath and have been taken out beforehand.)
Jesus gives more advice, clearly for Jews - when you see the abomination in the temple it is time to flee, for the tribulation will now become the great tribulation.

It will be like the day of Noah. Everything had become so evil that God sent the flood. Noah and his family were the only ones saved. They were taken out of the flood (the wrath and punishment of God) to a place of safety – in the ark. Similarly the church are removed from the wrath of God and punishment of a very sinful world in the tribulation, at the rapture – being taken to the place Jesus has prepared as spoken of in John 14.

Through Matthew gives the Jews more notice of this coming event in verse 37-44. Two working in a field, two grinding at a mill - one is taken and the other left. This is the rapture - the one taken is delivered from the wrath to come, same principle as with Noah.
Now Jesus says, watch, *'you do not know what hour your Lord is coming.'* (Watch out here – The NIV and other translations change the Greek *hora* hour to *hemera* day, one of many errors.)

Note – in verse 36 where Jesus said, 'of that day and hour no one knows,' He was speaking of the end of the tribulation when life on earth was far from normal. Whereas now He is speaking of the rapture. He likens it to the days of Noah when life on earth was continuing as normal for that time. He drops the word 'day' leaving only 'you do not know the hour.' This has to be so to allow the command and promise of 1 Thessalonians 5:5-11, 'you are sons of the light and sons of the day,' these things do not come upon us as a thief in the night so watch and be sober.

When the rapture comes to pass we could expect that many Jews will then be saved – they being familiar with the scriptures, will see that they have been left behind – many will turn to the Lord.

Too late to become part of the bride, they will go through the tribulation - those who endure to the end will populate Jesus millennial kingdom. (Along with many Gentiles who also turn to the Lord during the tribulation. Many are martyred during the tribulation.)

The signs

The rapture we have just discussed. Previously when answering the questions of the disciples – 'what will be the sign of Your coming?' was answered by Jesus parable of the fig tree.

Jesus said as a sign of His coming in Matthew 24, 'Look at the fig tree,' *added in Luke 'and all the trees,'* when you see them establishing and budding you know the time is near. Since 1933, when there were about 70 nations on earth, the number of 'trees' (nations) has now increased to over 200.

The fig tree is widely accepted as representing Israel which was brought back into existence in May 1948, since when it has flourished in the midst of its enemies.

As I write Israel is in an impossible position Having been invaded by Hamas, the rulers of Gaza, it is responding by trying to eliminate them. For a very short period most of the world supported Israel.

But very quickly that support drained away and we see the world in the process of turning away from Israel, thus fulfilling scripture. Today, January 2024, America is still supporting Israel. How long before its support is withdrawn?

At the end of the tribulation all the armies of the world assemble to fight Israel and the coming King Jesus, as recorded in Revelation 19.

Conclusions

The believing church will be aware of the coming rapture as Paul confirms to the Thessalonians

Be watchful as the time approaches

Don' fear the current tribulations in the world

There is still time to snatch some from the fire

The time is rapidly approaching for Jesus return

Chapter 7
The overview of time

A number of early church writers had the understanding that one day of creation from Genesis 1 represented 1,000 years for mankind on earth before eternity.

Written by Irenaeus for example:
'For in so many days as the world was made, in so many thousand years shall it be concluded ...... In six days created things were completed; it is evident that, therefore, they will come to an end after 6,000 years.'

The Epistle of Barnabas carries the same message as do the writings of Hippolytus. There are similar messages in other Jewish writings and in The Talmud.
The Apostle Peter confirmed the concept of one day representing 1,000 years in his second letter.

If that is correct then chapter 24 of Matthew would fit just before Jesus returns to establish the last 1,000 years spoken of in Revelation 20 – and clearly positioned at the end of the Great Tribulation.

That would mean mankind has already lived through almost all of the 6,000 years the early church writers expected.

The bible is full of information about times and years. A well known early cleric calculated that creation itself was 4004 BC - Bishop Usher. He did that by adding up all the stated lengths of reign of the Kings of Israel. We have clearly lived over 2,000 years AD since then.

Since his day we have much more understanding of how God counts time and have been able to account exactly for the time before Christ - BC.

The time after Christ is common knowledge as we count our years in reference to His birth.

Exact details are beyond the scope of this study but are available in various booklets:
The story of time
The way of the moon and the way of the sun
The Lamb of God
Last Orders
Ostrich Christianity

.. all have various details.

Our conclusion is that we could be very close to the return of Jesus to collect His bride, the tribulation, and the return of Jesus to reign for 1,000 years.
As the first 6,000 years have been accounted for exactly and literally the 1,000 years coming reign is certain.

Other titles:
The   ICCC – Transformed Working Life series:
Inherent Power
Work is a 1st class calling
No one can serve two masters
Hope - the certainty of future blessing
Faith or presumption
Hearing God speak
Working from rest
Renewing the mind
Be strong in the battle
Anointing
Fruitfulness
Other booklets written for ICCC
Powered by grace
Works of power - now is the time
Stand tall - take your position
Transformed Working Life - quick view

Other publications
Will the church be caught away?
Explaining the future.
Rightly dividing the word of truth.
So that's what it's all about   (overview of the bible
account)
*Daniel (introductory level)
*Revelation (introductory level)
Ostrich Christianity
Israel and the church not in competition
Favour - enjoying the children's bread.
What should we do with money?
Going for Gold – the testing and stretching of our faith
After Brexit – the nature of the battle ahead

Last Orders
Wisdom
The King is coming
Health and Healing
The sign of Jonah – solved
Understanding the parable of the 10 virgins
The Kingdom Way
The Persistent Widow
Can I lose my salvation?
Meet the Teacher
Love, 153 fish and seven signs
Paul's thorn in the flesh - its message for today
Deception and how to avoid it
Chosen and Choice
The end is not quite yet
Amazing numbers
Blood – the blood of the New Covenant
Building spiritual strength
Grace and judgement
The believer's authority
God's eternal purpose
And God spoke - hearing God speak today
Understanding Hebrews
Reigning in life
Inspiration from Word for the week
Jesus said Watch
Creation? Evolution? Difficult to choose.
Made in God's image – why and what does it
mean
Grace and peace from the seven spirits
Jesus and the feasts
Practical spiritual warfare
Sons, children, servants

Qumran 7
Parables
Oil and wine
James and the meaning of faith
Demolishing strongholds
Is the bible reliable?
The story of time
The way of the moon and the way of the sun
The fear of God and the love of God
Anxiety – keys to leaving anxiety behind
Jesus pathway through life
The two ordinances of Christianity

To access printed copies at Amazon - type peter
michell in the search box.
* Not in print

All booklets are available as free PDF downloads at
www.freebiblebooklets.com

Printed in Great Britain
by Amazon

36454290R00020